NOW YOU CAN READ ABOUT....
CREATURES of the DEEP

TEXT BY HARRY STANTON

ILLUSTRATED BY COLIN NEWMAN

BRIMAX BOOKS • NEWMARKET • ENGLAND

This is a sailfish. It has a fin
like a sail on top of its body.
This fin stops the fish from
rolling over when it races through
the water. Sailfish can swim at
speeds of up to one hundred
kilometres an hour.

The swordfish
can also swim
very fast. It uses
its sword when
hunting smaller
fish.

There are many different
kinds of shark. The largest
is the whale shark. It is the
largest fish in the sea.
Whale sharks can only eat
very tiny creatures which
they find in the sea.

The great white
shark is very
dangerous. It has
powerful jaws and
rows of sharp
teeth. When a shark
loses a tooth it
grows another one.

Rays are flat
fish which seem
to fly through
the water.

Rays are very difficult to see.
They can change colour to match
the sea bed.

The electric ray
can catch its
prey by giving it
an electric shock.

The sting ray
has a long whip-
like tail. With
this tail it stings
its enemies.

Whales are not fish. They are animals which live in the sea. They are not fish because they cannot breathe under water.

Blue whales are the largest creatures in the world. A fully grown blue whale weighs as much as fifteen elephants.

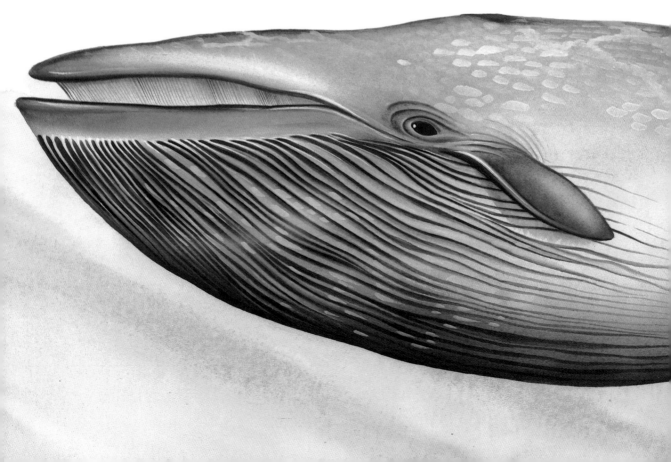

Dolphins often follow
ships as they sail
along. They race through
the water leaping
over the waves.

Eels are long
thin fish
found in
rivers, ponds
and the sea.

A squid is like a
small octopus. Squid
swim by drawing
in water, then squirting
it out behind them.

An octopus has eight
long arms. When it is
frightened an octopus
will squirt out a cloud
of black ink.

In the very deepest parts of the
sea it is dark and cold. Some very
strange fish live there.
Some of these
fish shine
like lamps in
the dark.

The deep sea angler
fish uses the light
to catch smaller fish.

The ugly gulper eel has thin pointed teeth in its enormous mouth.

Another fish with lights is the deep sea dragon. They run along its sides. Hanging from its chin is a long thin line.

With its long nose
the file fish looks
for food between
the rocks. Its skin
is so rough that
carpenters can use
it as sand paper.

The moorish idol fish also has a
long nose. It has strong jaws and
many teeth.

This brightly coloured
fish is called a
butterfly fish.

Another brightly coloured
fish is the angel fish. Just
behind its eyes it has a very
sharp spike. This helps stop
other fish from eating it.

Here is a sun fish.
The sun fish lives
near the surface
of the sea.

Sea horses do not
look like any other
fish. They cannot
swim very fast. Often
they hang on to
seaweed with their tails.

When flying fish are frightened, they leap from the sea and glide away from their enemies.

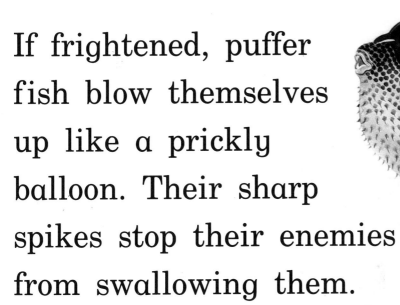

If frightened, puffer fish blow themselves up like a prickly balloon. Their sharp spikes stop their enemies from swallowing them.

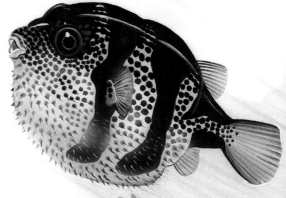

Brightly coloured tropical fish
can be kept in an aquarium. The
water has to be kept warm. A pump
is used to put fresh air into
the water.

Goldfish can be
kept in an
unheated aquarium.
The plants in
an aquarium help
to keep the
water fresh.

In this book you have read about all these fish. What are their names?

Swordfish

Puffer

Blue Whale

Moorish Idol

Squid

Sea Horse

Electric Ray

Deep Sea Dragon

Angel Fish

File Fish

Sunfish

Gulper Eel

Sailfish

Deep Sea Angler

Flying Fish

Butterfly Fish

Octopus

White Shark